Knights of Jericho

The English Revised Ritual of the Knights of Jericho

Knights of Jericho

The English Revised Ritual of the Knights of Jericho

ISBN/EAN: 9783337286606

Printed in Europe, USA, Canada, Australia, Japan

Cover: Foto ©Andreas Hilbeck / pixelio.de

More available books at **www.hansebooks.com**

" HUMANITY, TEMPERANCE AND CHARITY,"

THE ENGLISH

REVISED

RITUAL

OF THE

KNIGHTS OF JERICHO.

PREPARED BY A COMMITTEE

APPOINTED BY AND ACTING UNDER

AUTHORITY OF THE GRAND LODGE OF GEORGIA,

CONTAINING A SYNOPSIS OF

THE CEREMONIAL RIGHTS OF THE ORDER.

REVISED BY THE GRAND CHIEF.

APPROVED, Atlanta, November, 1874.

Test:
W. J. WARLICK, Grand Secretary.

HOKE SMITH, Grand Chief.

ATLANTA, GEORGIA :
SOUTHERN PUBLISHING CO., BOOK AND JOB PRINTERS.
1874.

INTERIOR VIEW OF A LODGE.

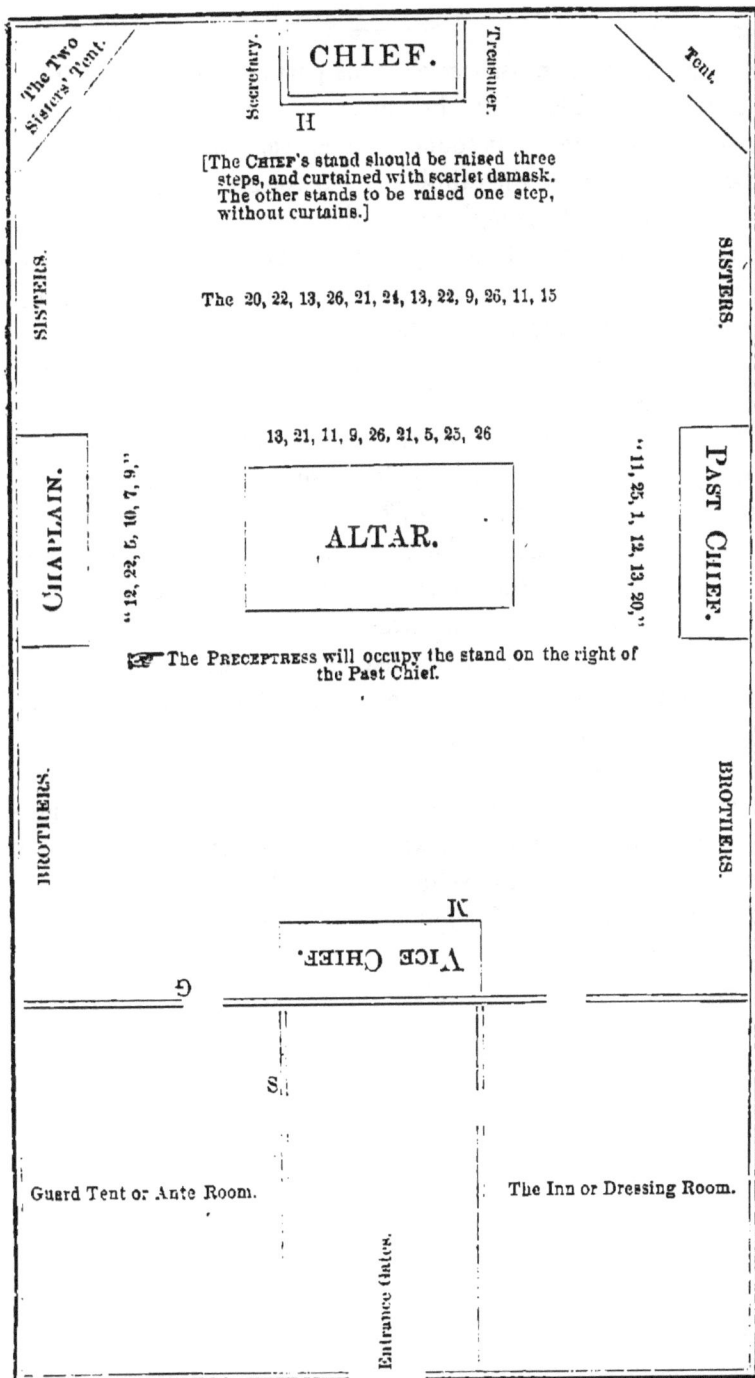

The Two Sisters' Tent.

Secretary.

CHIEF.

II

Treasurer.

Tent.

[The CHIEF's stand should be raised three steps, and curtained with scarlet damask. The other stands to be raised one step, without curtains.]

SISTERS.

The 20, 22, 13, 26, 21, 24, 13, 22, 9, 26, 11, 15

SISTERS.

13, 21, 11, 9, 26, 21, 5, 25, 26

CHAPLAIN.

"12, 22, 5, 10, 7, 9,"

ALTAR.

"11, 25, 1, 12, 13, 20,"

PAST CHIEF.

☞ The PRECEPTRESS will occupy the stand on the right of the Past Chief.

BROTHERS.

BROTHERS.

K

VICE CHIEF.

G

S

Guard Tent or Ante Room.

The Inn or Dressing Room.

Entrance Gates.

RULES.

1. Each officer must *memorize* his part as soon after his installation as possible; but he must not repeat it *as if from memory*. The nearer it sounds like extemporizing, the more impressive it will be to the candidate. A solemn and stately motion must be observed throughout all the ceremonies. Every word in each lecture should have the weight of a prayer. Not only must all levity be strictly forbidden, but the profoundest gravity should be cultivated by the officiating Chief.

2. It is indispensable that the brothers and sisters occupy the positions assigned them in the diagram annexed.

3. It shall be discretionary with females whether they be simply obligated or regularly initiated. If only obligated, let them be seated near the Vice Chief's stand during the initiation.

4. A National Lodge, having proved expensive, and otherwise objectionable, the private work of every kind shall be printed *only* by order of the Grand Lodge.

5. It is earnestly recommended that a choir, composed of the best vocalists of both sexes, be organized in each Lodge, and that instrumental music be introduced on all proper occasions.

6. The Chief is responsible for the safe keeping of the private work of the Lodge. At the close of each meeting each officer must deposit his hand-book with him, or procure his consent to let it be retained not exceeding one month.

7. All Subordinate Lodges shall receive all Grand and Past Grand Officers with the usual honors.

☞ For Regalia, Insignias and Emblems, see Appendix.

GRAND OFFICERS' TITLES.

1. The Sir Knight Grand Chief.
2. The Sir Knight Grand Vice Chief.
3. The Sir Knight Grand Chaplain.
4. The Sir Knight Grand Secretary.
5. The Sir Knight Grand Marshal.
6. The Sir Knight Grand Guard.
7. The Sir Knight Junior Past Grand Chief.

SUB-OFFICERS' TITLES.

1. The Sir Knight Chief.
2. The Sir Knight Vice Chief.
3. The Lady Preceptress.
4. The Sir Knight Chaplain.
5. The Sir Knight Secretary.
6. The Sir Knight Treasurer.
7. The Sir Knight Marshal.
8. The Sir Knight Herald.
9. The Sir Knight Guard.
10. The Sir Knight Sentinel.
11. The Sir Knight Junior Past Chief.

PRINCIPLES.

To God we owe Obedience, Love and Worship; to the world, Justice; to our brethren, Forgiveness and Fraternity; to ourselves, Sustenance and Protection.

Motto: Humanity, Temperance and Charity.

OPENING.

☞ 1. The time having arrived, the Chief will take the Chair, and call to order by giving one loud rap with the gavel.

HERALD. (Standing.) *Officers, Sir Knights, and Sisters,* ATTENTION ! The Chief is now about to open———— Lodge Knights of Jericho, by authority of the Grand Lodge of————. If there be any present not justly entitled to remain, they will please retire. The officers will repair to their posts, and hold themselves in readiness for further orders. Let there be silence during the examination.

☞ 2. The Secretary will call the roll of officers, and note absentees. The Chief fills vacancies, and says :

CHIEF. Sir Knight Guard, you have been detailed as an officer for this Lodge. What are the duties implied by your commission ?

GUARD. To guard the inner gate, permit none to enter during the opening or closing ceremonies, nor at any time, unless proper signals and countersigns are given, except by order of the Chief; permit no one to pass out unless they have first given the sign, and obtained permission from the Chief to retire ; and to faithfully discharge such other duties as the Constitution and By-Laws may require.

CHIEF. You have said well, Sir Knight Guard. Yours is an important post and duty. Guard well the one, and discharge promptly and faithfully the other, that you may merit the promotion by which the brave and vigilant soldier is rewarded by his comrades. You will advance and satisfy me that you are correct in the countersigns. . . Correct, Sir Knight. Return to your post, and remember that if yours is the post of danger, it is also the post of honor.

☞ 3. The Guard will give one rap and raise the wicket, when the Sentinel will present himself, and satisfy the Guard that he is correct in the Nazarite, or permanent countersign.

GUARD. Sir Knight Chief, the Sentinel is on duty, properly armed and correctly instructed.

CHIEF. Sir Knights Marshal and Herald, the Guard and Sentinel being at their posts well armed and with proper instructions, you will now proceed to examine all present in the semi-annual and permanent countersigns, and report to me all who cannot satisfy you of their right to remain.

☞ 4. The Marshal beginning on the right of the Vice Chief and ending on the left of the Chief, and the Herald beginning on the left of the Vice Chief and ending on the right of the Chief, will examine all present, advance to the altar, salute the Chief and report.

MARSHAL, (gives sign). Sir Knight Chief, all's well on your left.

HERALD, (gives sign). All's well on your right, Sir Knight Chief.

CHIEF, (calls up). Officers, Sir Knights and Sisters, we have assembled for the transaction of all such business appertaining to this Order as shall legally and properly come before us. In our deliberations, let our language and deportment be in harmony with our high and noble motto—Humanity, Temperance and Charity—that we may work in harmony, live in peace, and practice those great cardinal principles inculcated by our Order.

MEMBERS. So may we ever work and live.

CHIEF. We will sing the ——— Ode.

1st. OPENING ODE—AIR "Sweet Home."

Almighty Jehovah,
Descend now and fill
This Lodge with Thy glory—
Our hearts with good will.

Preside at our meetings,
Assist us to find
True pleasure in teaching
Good will to mankind.

CHORUS:

Home, home, sweet, sweet home ;
Prepare us, dear Saviour,
For glory, our home.

2d ODE—AIR "Coronation."—*Melbourne.*

How good and how pleasant 'tis for all
In unity to live;
On such the dew of Heav'n shall fall,
And holy love shall thrive.

Then let one object fill each heart,
One cause each spirit move ;
Thus shall we nobly act our part,
And smiling Heav'n approve.

☞ 5. The Chaplain will lead in prayer, after the 1st or 2d Ode shall
have been sung.

CHIEF. By authority of the Grand Lodge of ———, and by
virtue of my office, I now declare this Lodge open and ready to
transact any business that may lawfully come before it. (*Calls
down.*)

INITIATION.

☞ 6. As soon as the balloting for candidates is over, the Chief will call to order, and say:

CHIEF. Sir Knight Herald, you will retire to the ante-room and see if any one is in waiting to become a member of this Lodge "Knights of Jericho."

☞ 7. The Herald will retire, and, on his return, give the usual salutations, and report as he finds. If any, he will say:

H. Sir Knight Chief, I find ———— in waiting.

CHIEF. Sir Knight Herald, you will again retire, prepare the candidate, and bring ———— in for examination. Sir Knight Guard, you will let them pass and repass.

☞ 3. The Herald 6,25,25,10,17,5,26,3,21 and brings in the candidate, and proceeds directly to the Vice Chief's stand, and says:

H. Sir Knight Vice Chief, I have in charge————, who wishes to enlist as a volunteer in the grand army of moral reform, and————now most respectfully requests that you will make the necessary examination.

V. C. Respected————: you are welcome to the threshold of our Lodge, the sanctuary of Honor and Justice. But before you proceed further, justice to you demands that we should make known our Principles, and to us, that they receive your cordial assent; otherwise, it will be impossible for you to advance a step beyond this examination.

Our Order was instituted for the purpose of associating men and women together as brothers and sisters, and enabling them to live as such; encouraging each other to walk in the paths of Virtue and Honor, and to afford *material* aid in the hours of adversity. To secure ourselves from the intrusion of those who are unworthy, the forms and ceremonies which you will this night witness have been adopted.

Do you acknowledge the existence of an Almighty God, the Supreme Ruler of the Universe, to whom we are all accountable here and hereafter, and the divinity of the Lord Jesus Christ? [I do.]

In the presence of that great and good Being, are you willing to enter into a solemn covenant with the brothers and sisters of this Order, to abstain from, and discourage the use, as a beverage, of all intoxicating liquors during your connection with the Order, and so conduct yourself through life as to retain your good name, and not bring the Order into disrepute; and that you will conform to the Constitution, Laws and Regulations of the Order, and do all that within you lies to sustain and carry out the same? [I am.]

You will now retire with the Herald, and wait the pleasure of the Chief.

☞ 9. The Herald and candidate withdraw directly to the ante-room, where the 12,13,26,10,13,7,9 is removed from his or her 9,15,9,21. As soon as the door is closed after them, the Vice Chief will rise and say.

V. C. Sir Knight Chief, I have examined the candidate, and find —— worthy to enter the gates of our Order, and —— is ready and willing to proceed.

CHIEF (*calls up*). Officers, Brothers and Sisters: We are now about to proceed with the important service of Initiation. All will observe strict decorum, under penalty of the By-Laws, or prompt and severe reprimand. (*Calls down.*) Prepare for the reception of the candidate.

☞ 10. Place a 20,9,26,20 from six to ten feet square (according to the capacity of the hall), made of some thick, dark-colored cloth, so that the light cannot be seen through it, in the corner of the hall, on the left of the Chief; let there be a small table with glasses and a bottle on it; also, a 21,20, 19,8,8,9,10,8,5,7,19,22,9, representing a 1,13,26, leaning on the table or coun-ter, and two members slightly disguised—one representing a liquor-seller, and the other his customer—sitting within as though engaged in a carousal. Remove the altar, if it be in the way, from the centre of the hall, and extinguish all the lights, except that in the 20,9,26,20, the 10,25,25,22 of which must be kept closed until the Marshal and candidate have gone once round the hall, when it must be partially opened, so as to emit a little light. Place the 12,22, 5,10,7,9 and balls of wood on the floor, near the Chaplain's stand. Let it be some twelve feet long, and so constructed that the front legs will give way and cause the rear end to tilt up when on top, and thereby cast off the rollers and balls—made to rise in the middle some two feet, and in two parts ; one end of each part rests on the floor, the other ends come together, and make the rise something like a 2,13,10,10,9,22 cut in two pieces, only that the rollers are dropped in notches cut on the top, so that it will tumble to pieces. The rear end should be some two feet the longest, so that the front legs will give way. Let the balls be large, and the rollers some two feet long and two inches in diameter. When everything is ready, the Vice Chief will say :

V. C. Sir Knight Chief, everything is now in readiness for the Initiation.

CHIEF. Sir Knight Guard, you will give the alarm; if answered without by the Herald, throw open the gate and let them enter.

☞ 11 The Guard gives one loud rap on the door. The Herald, in the ante-room, answers by giving two raps, when the Guard will raise the wicket, and say :

G. Who comes there ?

H. The Herald, with a stranger, who is traveling eastward as far as Jericho.

G. Is he true and trusty ?

H. He has been tried and found worthy.

G. Enter; and bear in mind that you are surrounded on every hand by difficulties and dangers.

☜ 12. The Herald and candidate having entered, and the door closed, the Marshal will 20,13,3,9 the candidate by 12,25,20,6-21,6,25,19,2,10,9,22,21, and say, " Hold !" etc. The Marshal will retain one very dim light near the door until he and the candidate commence their journey, when it must be extinguished.

M. Hold! presumptuous mortal! What brings you here upon this sacred ground? Who are you?—and what is your business here? (*Not violently.*)

H. Sir Knight Marshal, you will not treat my friend unkindly; his business this way is most praiseworthy. Although not yet a member of our Order, he is on his way to Jericho to be enrolled as a volunteer in the grand army of moral reform; and as I can go no further, into your charge I commit my worthy friend. He has already been informed of the great danger in traveling, but he is bold and courageous. (*Takes ——by the hand.*) Good-bye; look sharp for the Star of Hope and Promise, and remember that Prayer is the bridge that spans from earth to Heaven. Farewell!

M. Stranger, I understand that your object is to reach Jericho in the shortest time possible. I will accompany you with pleasure, and render you all the assistance in my power. You see everything 12,9,8,**25,22**,9 you 2,25,25,3,21-10,13,22,3 and 7,2,25,25,1,15.

It requires stout hearts to travel this path. Now, let us 24, 19,20-25,26 our 24,13,11,3,21 containing 11,2,25,20,6,5,26,7 and 24,22,-25,18,5,21,5,25,26 for this 2,25,26,7 and 20,5,22,9,21, 25,1,4,25,19,22,26,9,15.

☞13. The Marshal adjusts the 3,26,13,24,21,13,11,3 on the candidate's 21,6,25,19,2,10,9,22,21, takes him or her by the arm and moves slowly round the hall, saying, as they proceed:

M. Stranger, we will now move on. We have a long and somewhat difficult travel before us; but

> The gloomy mantle of the night,
>   Which on our sinking spirits steals,
> Will vanish at the morning light,
>   Which GOD, our All, our Sun, reveals.

☞14. The Marshal will so time the delivery of the foregoing as to finish the sentence just as he has made the circuit of the hall. As he reaches the Vice Chief's stand, the noise within the 20,9,26,20 becomes boisterous. The customer will half-open the door, and commence, "I say, Mr. Tapster, I want another drink, I does." Tapster—"Well, have you got the money?" Customer—"I am good for a drink—say, ain't I?" Tapster—"Not another drop without the money." "What! after I have spent all my money with you? Well, now, that do settle it." The Marshal stops suddenly, and addresses the candidate in a low, quick, earnest manner:

M. Stranger, be brave—fear not. The noise you hear emanates from that miserable 7,22,25,7-21,6,25,24, the like of which, alas! are too frequently to be met with in our cities, villages, and even in our quiet rural districts. That 10,9,26 is kept by a notorious vagabond, who is known to the people around by the name of the 22,19,1-8,5,9,26,10. Several 1,19,22,10,9,22, 21 have been committed on and about his premises, and many hearths made desolate. Brothers and sisters, parents and children, husbands and wives, neighbors, lovers, and friends mourn over his numerous 18,5,11,20,5,1,21. Hearts have been crushed and made to bleed; honest laborers stripped of their last hard-earned dollar; widows and orphans turned out penniless and shelterless upon the cold charities of the world, and the virtuous and respectable despoiled of a stainless reputation, and covered with a cloud of infamy, through his infernal agency! Still, he goes unwhipped of Justice—no 2,9,7,13-24,22,25,25,8 having yet been obtained against him. Our path leads directly past his 10,9,26. We will push on cautiously, so as to avoid observation (*they go forward*), and trust to Divine Providence for the result.

☞ 15. As the Marshal and candidate arrive near the Past Chief's stand, the noise within the 20,9,26,20 is increased—the parties quarrel, something after this manner: Customer—"I say, Mr. Tapster, I will have another drink, I will." Tapster—"Not another drop until you have paid for what you have got." Customer—"I will have another drink! you old rascal—villian, that you are!" Tapster—"Don't you call me a villian, you good-for-nothing vagabond; get out of my shop, or I will put you out!" etc. The 10,25,25,22 is thrown open, and the 8,5,7,19,22,9 is thrown outside, and falls heavily on the floor, at which moment a deep 7,22,25,13,26 is uttered by the brother who throws it out. The Marshal and candidate stop. The lights inside the 20,9, 26,20 are quickly extinguished, and the two who were inside go up to the 11,25,22,24,21,9. One will say in a whisper, "6,9,5,21-10,9,13,10—I didn't mean to 3,5,2,2 him—help me 10,22,13,7 him near the 24,19,12,2,5,11-22,25

13,10, along which some of those Knights of Jericho must 24,13,21,21 to-night on their way 6,25,1,9.   They then 10,22,13,7 the 8,5,7,19,22,9 across the room, and leave it in the front of the Chief's stand, and run quickly across the hall to the left of the Vice Chief, where they quietly take seats.   During the whole of this scene the Marshal and candidate remain standing, as if lost in bewilderment.   When the two who were with the 8,5,7,19,22,9 are seated, the Marshal, with some signs of agitation, says:

M. They have no doubt 3,5,2,2,9,10 that poor fellow, and intend 11,25,26,11,9,13,2,5,26,7 his 12,25,10,15, so as to 6,5, 10,9, all 20,22,13,11,9,21 of their 7,19,5,2,10.   Oh, Intemperance! what a prolific source of crime and misery thou art! Let us pursue the villians, and endeavor to bring them to 4,19, 21,20,5,11,9.

☞ 16. The Marshal and candidate push on quickly, and the latter is made to stumble against the 8,5,7,19,22,9.   They stop, and the Marshal stoops down and discovers it, when he exclaims, "It is the poor 17,22,9,20,11,6 who was doubtless 1,19,32,10,9,22,9,10 by those villains a short distance back. 6,9, 2,24-25-12,22,5,26,7-1,9-6,9,2,24!"   At this moment the Herald approaches from the corner of the hall with a small 2,13,26,10,9,22,26, which, until then, has been concealed.   When he gets near them, affecting not to see any one— he says:

H. I thought I heard the cry of some one in deep distress. Could I have been mistaken?

M. No, my friend, you are not mistaken.   It was I who called for help.   Here 2,5,9,21 the 2,5,8,9,2,9,21,21-12,25,10,15 of a poor victim of (I dare say) that old villain, 22,19,1-8,5,9, 26,10.   As I passed his 10,9,26, in company with my friend here, we heard high and angry words.   We saw some one thrust from the 7,22,25,7,7,9,22,15, and thought we heard something said by one of the party like a confession of 1,19,22,10,9,22. You will please take charge of the 11,25,22,24,21,9, and permit myself and friend to pass on.   We are on our way to Jericho, and fear we shall not reach there before the 7,13,20,9,21 are closed.

H. You can proceed on your way.   You have no time to lose.   Good-bye.

M. Good-bye—God bless you. (*To the Candidate.*) My friend, there can be no doubt that the 5,26,13,26,5,1,13,20,9-8,25,22,1 we have just seen is that of the poor fellow who was so rudely expelled from the 7,22,25,7,7,9,22,15 we passed a short distance back. I beseech you, be warned by his 21,13,10-8,13, 20,9. Remember for what purpose you were created, and through the whole of your future life, look at its end, and consider, when that comes, in what you will put your trust. Not in the bubbles of worldly vanity—they will be broken; not in worldly pleasures —they will be gone; not in wealth—you cannot carry it with you; not in rank—in the grave there is no distinction ; not in the recollection of a life spent in a giddy conformity to the silly fashions and customs of a thoughtless and wicked world; but in that of a life spent soberly, righteously and Godly in this present world. [The members will say, "11,13,18,9! 11,13, 18,9!" pronounced 3,18.] Stranger, be brave; fear not—ours is a righteous cause. We will push on, and trust to Divine Providence for the result. This 10,13,22,3,26,9,21,21 will only serve to make the 2,5,7,6,20 more glorious.

☞ 17. The Marshal w ll so time the delivery of the foregoing as to finish before reaching the 12,22,5,10,7,9, and having 11,22,25,21,21,9,10, the Marshal and candidate face towards the Chief's stand and 10,5,21,11,25,18,9,22 the 21,20,13,22. The Marshal says "Hold! Hold!" etc. The members 11,2, 13,24-20,6,9,5,22-6,13.26,10,21. Tho Marshal continues, "Heaven be praised!" eto., when the third Ode will be sung. (The 6,13,2,2 must be perfectly 10,13, 22,8.) As soon as the singing is over, the Marshall conducts the candidate near the 20,22,13,26,21,24,13,22,9,26,11,15, or seats him in front of the Vice Chief's stand, until all the candidates are taken through the preceding scene, and then bring all before it, and then withdraw to the ante-room and return.

M. Hold! Hold ! Thank Heaven that we are permitted to behold the Star of Hope and Promise. (Hall to the Brightness!) Heaven be praised! we are saved, and soon shall be delivered from darkness. Nothing short of Divine Providence can prevent our reaching Jericho.

3d ODE—Star of Bethlehem.

When marshalled on the mighty plain,
　　The glittering host bestud the sky;
One Star alone, of all the train,
　　Can fix the sinner's wandering eye.

Hark! Hark! to God the chorous breaks,
　　From every host, from every gem;
But one alone the Saviour speaks,
　　It is the Star of Bethlehem?

☞ 18. If there are more candidates than one to be initiated, they must each be taken through the preceding scene separately, and seated in front of the Vice Chief's stand, until they are all advanced, and then proceed on. The Marshal and candidate walk very slowly once round the hall, stopping directly before the 20,22,13,26,21,24,13,22,9,26,11,15—which must be suspended in an upright case, or over a skeleton 11,25,8,8,5,26, with strong lights under or behind it. During the whole of this scene, let all the lights in the hall, except those necessary to give effect to the 20,22,13,26,21,24,13, 22,9,26,11,15, be extinguished. As soon as the Marshal and candidate leave the Vice Chief's stand—while going to the 20,22,18,26,21,24,13,22,9,26,11,15 —the Vice Chief will commence slowly and solemnly, twelve times, to imitate the 20,25,2,2,5,26,7 of a large 12,9,2,2 (which can be counterfeited by holding up a new 17,9,9,10,5,26,7-6,25,9, suspended by a 21,20,22,5,26,7, and striking it with his 7,18,18,9,2). When the 20,25,2,2,5,26,7 ceases, the Marshal will sing or repeat

4th ODE—Air, "Bethel."

Hark! from the tombs a doleful sound,
　　My ears attend the cry.
Ye living men, come view the ground
　　Where you must shortly lie.

Princes, this clay must be your bed,
　　In spite of all your towers;
The tall, the wise, the reverend head,
　　Must lie as low as ours.

☞ 19. The 4th Ode having been concluded, the Chaplain will proceed, speaking in a low and distinct manner. so as to give the utmost solemnity to his lecture:

CHAP.   You behold before you, in this 6,13,7,7,13,22,10-21, 3,9,2,9,20,25,26, a striking lesson of Man's mortality; remem-

ber that this is the unalterable fate of mortal man! We are all
fast hastening to that fearful state. Let this be a warning to
you to be prepared for that dreadful moment when you shall be
called upon to make that awful change; for we know not when
the day or hour cometh!

M. My friend, this has been to us a very eventful night. I
am sure the remembrance of it will not soon be obliterated from
my mind. But we now come to Gilgal, and as our provisions
are getting short, perhaps we had better stop at the inn and re-
fresh ourselves, and again push on [22,9,1,25,18,9, the 24,13,11,
3.] But stay; I had better give you the password, as it will
be required of you at every station you pass. Gives ["5-6,13,
18,9-21,9,9,26 the 21,20,13,22."] Stranger, we have been very
much rested; we now move on, determined to reach Jericho.
Our greatest troubles are over; we will put our trust in God
and fear no danger; but while we are traveling through this
dark valley, why not contemplate and consider our destiny here
and hereafter? It is a subject I delight to dwell upon. Stranger, I have seen a flower open it leaves to the rising sun; it
looked gay—it was beautiful to behold—its fragrance was de-
lightful; I sought it again, and lo! it had withered on the stem
that supported it. I have seen man in his youth; he looked
gay and was sprightly, and rejoiced that he had more life than
the flower. I have sought him again, and lo! he had gone the
way of all the earth; for all that is born must die, and that is
created must come to an end. Thus it is with mankind—to-
day in full health and vigor—their eyes sparkling with anima-
tion, and expecting to have many years allotted to them here in
this world, both of joy and sorrow; but to-morrow comes, and
those who were so gay but yesterday are now clothed in the
habiliments of the grave.

☞ 20. They go once round the hall, nearly to the stand of the Past Chief,
while the Marshal says:

M. Stop. [*The Herald will give a faint* 17,6,5,21,20,2,9,21
again.] I hear a whistle. This country is infested by thieves

A

and ruffians. Remain quiet. I will beat them off. I am well armed.

H. [*Approaching the Marshal.*] Your 1,25,26,9,15 or your 2,5,8,9!

M. [*Draws his sword.*] Away, you villains! [*A fight ensues.*] Villains, I will shoot you!

H. Hold! don't shoot! [The P. C. throws three or four large torpedoes over, so as to fall on the floor and burst. The H. brings one loud scream, drops his sword and runs off.]

☞ 21. After the engagement, the Marshal goes to the candidate, takes his or her arm, and says:

M. [*Apparently excited.*] I have given those villains a lesson which I hope will teach them better manners hereafter. Here we come to the first station.

☞ 22. They stop before the stand of the Past Chief, who says:

P. C. Who comes there?

M. A friend, who is on —— way to Jericho.

P. C. I demand the password. [*The candidate gives it.*] Have you met with any difficulty on your way?

M. We were attacked by some ruffians a short distance back, but soon put them to flight.

P. C. I am glad you gave those villains, who thus lay in wait to disturb our friends, a proper chastisement. You may proceed on your way; you will not again be disturbed. The distance is very short. You have only one more station to pass, at which you will find a worthy clergyman, who has always some pleasant word for the traveler. Good-bye!

M. [*Approaching the Chaplain's stand.*] Here we come to the second station.

CHAP. Stop a moment, my friends. It is my duty to demand the password. [*The candidate gives it.*] You are traveling to Jericho, I presume? Have you had a pleasant journey
thus far?

M. Except a little interruption before we reached the first
station, by a set of ruffians. ·

CHAP. You will always find more or less trouble in passing
through life.

> The path of sorrow, and that path alone,
> Leads to the land where sorrow is unknown;
> No traveler ever reached that blessed abode,
> Who found not thorns and briars in his road.

Receive this 12,5,12,2,9. [*Gives —— a small* 12,5,12,2,9.]
It shall be a lamp unto thy feet and a light unto thy path.
Good-bye. God bless you!

M. We thank you, sir. [*Moves forward.*] That man of
God has wisely admonished us; and our highest appreciation of
the gift will be a strict observance of all its rules.

☞ 23. The Herald will strike nine times on a 21,1,13,2,2-12,9,2,2. or 20,22,
5,13,26,7,2,9; at which time the Marshal will stop and say 25,26,9—20,17,25—
20,6,22,9,9—8,25,19,22—8,5,18,9—21,5,16—21,9,18,9,26—9,5, 7, 6, 20—26, 5,
26,9.

M. Hold! we now come to the extreme outer gate. It is 9
o'clock. The Sentinels and their families are assembling for
their evening devotions, and will not molest us. We will pass
on quietly to the city, which is not far off. The gates will not
be closed until 10 o'clock. [*In a low tone of voice.*] Hark!
what do we hear? It is heavenly music. ·

5th ODE—AIR, "Peterborough."—*Zerah.*

> Oh! praise the Lord with hymns of joy,
>   And celebrate his fame;
> For pleasant, good and comely 'tis
>   To praise his holy name.

CHAP. The rich and the poor meet together; the Lord is the the maker of them all. Blessed is he that considereth the poor: the Lord will deliver him in time of trouble." "The fear of the Lord is the beginning of knowledge: but fools despise wisdom and instruction." "All things whatsoever ye would that men should do to you, do ye even so to them; for this is the law and the prophets."

M. My friend, let the impressive lessons you have just heard ever remain fresh in your memory. Endeavor to emulate the example of these good people, and let your light so shine before men, that they, seeing your good works, may be induced to emulate you. But we are now in the presence of the Chief.

☞ 24. The Marshal and candidate are suddenly arrested in their progress, near the Chief's stand, by the Herald, who says:

H. Hold! What is your business here?

M. Do not delay us. I have important business with the Chief.

C. Who are you, and what is your business with me at this late hour?

M. Sir Knight Chief, I am the Marshal of this Lodge, and have in charge a friend who has been found worthy to enter within these walls, for the purpose of becoming a member of the noble Order of Knights of Jericho.

C. Stranger! you have gained admittance within these sacred walls for the purpose of becoming a ———— among brothers and sisters. We are endowed with the privilege emanating from the sovereignty of this Order, to perform all initiations coming before us, and are happy in performing this pleasing duty in the presence of Almighty God, and with feelings of the greatest kindness towards you.

I have a few questions to propound, and upon your answers will depend your further progress. Have you the recruiting password? [*Answer, "I have."*] I demand it. [*The candidate gives it.*] Is it your fixed purpose to labor in the cause of Humanity, Temperance and Charity? [*Answer, "It is."*] Brother Marshal, what further evidence have I that your friend is worthy?

M. He has this passport. [The "12,5,12,2,9."]

C. 'Tis enough. You will repair with the applicant to the altar. [*Calls up the officers.*]

☞ 25. The Marshal conducts the candidate once around the hall, to the altar, facing the Chief's stand, during which time the members sing the 6th Ode; after which he reports.

6th ODE—AIR, "Old Granite State."

Knights of Jericho are coming,
Knights of Jericho are coming,
Knights of Jericho are coming,
    With the cold water pledge;

Here's a band of brothers,
Here's a band of sisters,
Here's a band of brothers,
    In union sweet combined.

M. Sir Knight Chief, the candidate awaits your pleasure.

C. [*Calls the officers around the altar.*] The officers will gather around the altar, and assist me in administering the obligation.

PRE. My friend, I entreat you to consider well the step you are now about to take. The obligation you are required to enter into at this time is one of serious import, and cannot be violated without disgrace. It is one which we have all taken, and intend, with the help of God, to keep inviolate.

C. I appreciate your kindness, my sister. My friend, are you willing to proceed? [*Answer, "I am."*]

7th ODE—Air, "Old Hundred" [very low].

Before Jehovah's awful throne,
Ye nations bow with sacred joy;
Know that the Lord is God alone—
He can create, and He destroy.

C. My friend, you will 24,2,13,11,9-15,25,19,22-22,5,7,6,20-6,13,26,10-19,24,25,26-20,6,9-12,5,12,2,9, and repeat, after me, the following oath, first pronouncing your name:

I, ——, of my own desire, in this Lodge, Knights of Jericho, do most solemnly and sincerely promise, that I will obey the Constitution, Laws and regulations of the Grand Lodge, the By-Laws of this, or that of any other Lodge with which I may hereafter be in any manner connected; that I will abstain from and discourage the use, as a beverage, of all intoxicating liquors, during my connection with the Order, and so conduct myself through life as to retain my good name, and not bring the Order into disrepute; that I will never, in any manner, countenance, or consent to, the introduction of any person or persons of color as members of this Order; that I will cheerfully aid a worthy brother or sister, when in trouble or in need, if in my power so to do; and that I will not intentionally wrong or defraud this Order, or any member thereof. I do further promise that I will discourage vice and immorality, and cultivate a spirit of Humanity, Temperance and Charity in all the relations of life—especially with the brothers and sisters of this Order.

May God, in His infinite love and mercy, bless and enable me to keep and perform this, my solemn vow.

☞ 26. The Chief will 7,5,18,9 the 13,24,24,2,5,11,13,26,20 a 12,2,25,17 with 6,5,21,21,17,25,22,10 and say 22,5,21,9-21,5,22, you 13,22,9-19,26,10,9 22 the protection of brothers and sisters.

C. In the beginning God created the heavens and the earth, and the earth was without form and void; and darkness was upon the face of the deep; and God said let there be light and there was light.

☞ 28. As the last word above is uttered, the bandage must be removed from the eyes of the candidate.

C. My ———, on being brought to 2,5,7,6,20, your attention was first directed to the 21,17,25,22,10 and 12,5,12,2,9, which are placed upon the 13,2,20,13,22. You are doubtless anxious to know why they are placed here. I will explain to you their use.

The 21,17,25,22,10 is an implement of grim-visaged 17,13, 22; but we, as Knights of Jericho—the sworn foes of Intemperance, Immorality and Vice—have adopted it as an emblem of our Order. It will, likewise, serve to remind you of the vengeance of an offended God, which will certainly be visited upon you should you violate the solemn 25,12,2,5,7,13,20,5,25, 26 you have this night voluntarily taken.

As Knights of Jericho, we are taught to take this Book as our rule, guide and faith through life. Would you know its name? It is the "Book of Books:" its author, GOD: its theme, Heaven — Eternity! The BIBLE! Read it—search it, my ———. Let it be first upon the shelves of your library, and first in the affections of your heart. Search it; for if there be sublimity in the contemplation of God—if there be grandeur in the displays of Eternity—if there be anything ennobling and purifying in the revelation of Man's salvation—oh! search the Scriptures, for they are they which testify of these things.

The 10,13,22,3-21,11,9,26,9 through which you were required to pass, and the obstructions encountered on your way, were intended to remind you of the great uncertainty of human life, and your utter dependence on other than your own aid; for had not our worthy Marshal generously directed your steps, you might have found yourself in a sad predicament indeed!

Sir Knight Marshal, you will now introduce ——— to the Preceptress, after which you will return to me for further instructions.

☞ 27. The Chief will resume his seat, and the Marshal will conduct the candidates to the Preceptress, and after introducing him or her, the Preceptress will say:

PRE. [*Rises.*]　Hail, Knight or Lady of Jericho!
And be that name thy glory and thy shield.
High now is thy position
Among the sons and daughters of men —
Responsible and great
The duties it involves.
The foes of Temperance, and the friend alike,
Will look to your example,
And judge the cause by you :
Be faithful to the cause—the cause of all mankind—
　　Be faithful to yourself;
For all our laws require,
Tends to your lasting good.

> "Onward—a righteous cause is yours,
> 　And victory shall be won !
> Such zeal complete success insures,
> 　Go on, go on, go on.
>
> Onward—a thousand hearths shall smile,
> 　A thousand voices bless
> Your labor and your ceaseless toil,
> 　To save from wretchedness.
>
> Onward—a voice from Heaven cries,
> 　How melting is the tone :
> Methinks each sturdy heart replies,
> 　We will, we will go on !"

☞ 29. The Marshal and candidate go directly to the stand of the Chief, who, as soon as they reach there, rises and addresses the candidate as follows :

C.　My ――――: You have now taken an elevated position in the scale of honor, and are fully entitled to be made acquainted with the Grip, Test, Signs, Countersigns and other secrets of this Degree, with which you have not already been made acqainted. Remember that you have solemnly promised, in the presence of Almighty God, and the members here assembled, to keep sacred to the end of life all the secrets of this Order.

In order to obtain admittance into a Lodge, you will 1,13,3'
9-13,26,15-25,22,10,5,26,13,22,15-26,25,5,21,9 at the outer gate,
so as to attract the attention of the Sentinel, who is statioued in
the ante-room. To him you will give, in a whisper, the permanent Countersigu, when he will admit you. At the
second or inner gate you will give "20,6,22,9,9" distinct raps,
when the Guard will raise the wicket, and you will give him
the permanent and semi-annual password current within the
jurisdiction of the Grand Lodge of this ———, and he will
admit you. [*Give the word.*] Should you desire to visit any
Lodge of this Order, located in, and working under the jurisdiction of the Grand Lodge of any other State, you will report
that fact to the Guard, who will report the same to the Chief,
who will direct the Herald, or Marshal, to retire and make the
necessary examination, and introduce you to the Lodge when
fully satisfied.

On entering the Lodge, you will proceed to the 11,9,26,20,22,
9 of 20,6,9-6,13,2,2 near the 13,2,20,13,22 and salute the Chief
by giving him the second recognition sign, which is given in
this manner : Place your 25,24,9,26-2,9,8,20-6,13,26,10 on your
22,5,7,6,20-12,22,9,13,21,20, and at the same time 22,13,5,21,
9 the 22,5,7,6,20-6,13,26,10 as high as the top of the 9,13,22
and 24,25,5,26,20 the 5,26,10,9,16-8,5,26,7,9,22 upward; then
bring 12,25,20,6-6,13,26,10,21 to your 21,5,10,9-13,7,13,5,26,
when you will quietly take your seat. This sign signifies your
consciousness that the all-seeing eye of God is constantly watch-
ing your every action. The Chief will answer by returning the
sign, with 6,5,21-2,9,8,20-6,13,26,10, in the same manner.

The Grip is given by clasping the hand in the usual manner
of shaking hands, then press the 12,13,2,2 of the 20,6,19,1,12
against the 8,5,22,21,20-4,25,5,26,20 of the individual's 20,6,
19,1,12. The answer is given by returning the pressure in the
same manner. It may be that you will give this Grip to some
one who will return it without being, in fact, aware of its mean-
ing. You are not at liberty to take for granted that he or she
is a member, however, without first testing them, which must
be done by asking the one whom you wish to test, " Have you

20,22,13,18,9,2,9,10-1,19,1,1,6 ?" If they answer "15,9,21," or "5-6,13,18,9," then ask "6,25,17-8,13,22-6,13,18,9-15,25,19-12, 9,9,26 ?" The answer must be "To 4,9,22,5,11,6,25 ;" otherwise, let the examination cease.

The third, or true recognition sign is given by placing the 12, 13,2,2 of the 20,6,19,1,12 on the 26,13,5,2 of the 2,5,20,20,2, 9-8,5,26,7,9,22 of the 22,5,7,6,20-6,13,26,10, and then 22,13,5, 21,9, the 6,13,26,10 quickly, so as to let the 9,26,10,21 of the 20,6,22,9,9-8,5,26,7,9,22,21 touch the 20,25,24 of the 22,5,7,6, 20-21,6,25,19,2,10,9,22 casting the 6,13,26,10 off quickly, 24, 13,2,1 in 8,22,19,26,20 and quickly returning the hand to the side again—similar to that of a 1,5,2,5,20,13,22,15-21,13,2,19, 20,9. The answer is given with the 2,9,8,20-6,13,26,10 in the same manner.

The caution sign is given by 11,2,25,21,5,26,7 the 20,6,19, 1,12 over the 8,5,22,21,20,21,9,11,25,26,10 and 20,6,5,22,10-8, 5,26,7,9,22,21 of the 22,5,7,6,20-6,13,26,10. Then 10,22,13,17, the 9,26,10 of the 2,5,20,20,2,9-8,5,26,7,9,22 across directly 19, 26,10,9,22 the 22,5,7,6,20-9,15,9 say 20,6,22,9,9-20,5,1,9,21, in a careless manner. The Latin words to be used in lieu of, or as a substitute for the sign, are "11,13,18,9-11,13,18,9," pronounced "3,18-3,18." This sign or substitute is to be used to caution a brother or sister when they are about to go astray, and to guard them against imposition. Should either ever be given to you, it will be your duty to desist until you can have an interview with such a one.

These signs, etc., are never to be used outside of the Lodge room, except when you have some good object to accomplish. They must never be used frivolously, or for mere pastime.

It is also necessary that you should be instructed in the use of the *gavel*, which being the emblem of his authority, is used by the Chief to govern his Lodge. *One rap* of it will call the members to order, or seat them when standing; *two raps* will call up the officers only ; *three raps* will call up all the members ; and *four raps* will call up all the members around the 13,2,20, 13,22.

The Marshal will accompany you to the Secretary's desk, where you will sign our Constitution—after which he will instruct you how to work 'your way out and in the Lodge.

☞ 30. The Marshal takes the candidate first to the Secretary's desk, and after he or she has signed the Constitution, then to the ante-room, where he will teach him or her as directed. The Marshal will return to the Lodge in advance of the initiate, and accompany him or her to the 18-11, and 13,2,20, 13,22. When they have given the salutations, the Chief will call up the members around the altar, and go down.

C. My ———, you have now been fully instructed in the signs, etc., of this Degree. I now proclaim you a worthy member. Brothers and sisters, you will now extend to ——— the hand of fellowship, and treat ——— as a ———.

☞ 31. The members then pass slowly around the altar, shaking the hand of the new member as they proceed, while they sing the 8th Ode:

8th ODE—Air, "Sparkling and Bright."

———

Sparkling and bright with its liquid light
   Is the water in our glasses.
'Twill give you health, 'twill give you wealth,
   Ye lads and rosy lasses.
Oh, then resign your ruby wine,
   Each smiling son and daughter;
There's nothing so good for the youthful blood,
   Or sweet as the sparkling water!

☞ 32. Having made the circuit, the Chief calls down and proceeds with the regular business of the Lodge.

CLOSING.

CHIEF. Sir Knight Treasurer, you will please report the receipts of the evening.

☞ 33. The Treasurer reports the total amount received since last meeting.

C. Sir Knight Secretary, you will make a minute of the amount reported by the Treasurer.

SEC. I have made the record, Sir Knight Chief.

C. [*Calls up.*] We will sing the —— Ode.

9th ODE—AIR, "Ripley."

Now, Farewell! our banquet's over;
Heavenly blessings on us fall;
Farewell, sister—farewell, brother,
Farewell, loved ones—farewell, all!

Gracious Father! hear our pleading!
Gratitude our bosoms swell;
Guard us with Thy holy keeping;
Bless our parting word, farewell!

10th ODE—AIR, "Temperance."

Heavenly Father! give Thy blessing,
While we now this meeting end;
On our minds each truth impressing
That may to Thy glory tend.

Save from all intoxication,
From its fountain may we flee;
When assailed by strong temptation,
Put our trust alone in Thee!

CHAP. [Benediction.]

C. Officers, Sir Knights, and Sisters: Sincerely hoping that, after a pleasant and useful sojourn at Jericho, we may finally meet and be accepted in the Grand Lodge above, I now declare this Lodge closed until our next regular communication, unless called together by special emergency; in which case due notice will be given. Sir Knights and Sisters, farewell.

FUNERAL SERVICE.

1. When the members are called together to attend the funeral of a brother or sister, they shall meet at the Lodge room, where the Lodge will be opened in the Degree of Jericho. If more than one Lodge is engaged in the ceremonies, they shall proceed according to their rank in age and number, the youngest going first, except that the Lodge to which the deceased belonged shall go next to the hearse or litter. Should the deceased be a stranger or sojourner, the oldest Lodge in the city or town where he died, or, if in the country, the nearest Lodge shall take charge of the funeral. Uniformity in dress should be observed, as much as possible, by the members appearing in procession. If the deceased be a sister, the pall-bearers should be sisters; if a brother, they must be brothers. The sisters may meet, either with the brothers at the Lodge room, and march with them to the house of deceased, or they may meet at the house of deceased, without going to the Lodge room; the latter course is recommended. All must wear regalia in mourning. No member will be permitted to leave the ranks or desert their places, after the procession is formed, until dismissed. The following shall be the

ORDER OF PROCESSION:

Music.

G.—Banner in Mourning.—S.

Sisters, two abreast.

Brothers, two abreast.

Past Chiefs, two abreast.

Secretary and Treasurer.

Vice Chief and Herald, with rod.

Chief and Chaplain.

Pall-Bearer.	Pall-Bearer.
Pall-Bearer.	Pall-Bearer.
Pall-Bearer.	Pall-Bearer.

Mourners.

Immediate friends of deceased.

Citizens generally.

On arriving at the grave, the procession will halt and open to the right and left, and the corpse will be borne through it to the grave—the brothers standing uncovered until it passes. The Chief and Chaplain will take positions at the head of the grave, the other officers next, on each side, according to rank; the mourners at the foot, and the brothers and sisters forming a circle around them. As soon as the coffin is deposited in the grave, the brethren will again take off their hats and remain uncovered during the rehearsal of the following ceremony:

C. Man that is born of woman is of few days and full of trouble; he cometh forth like a flower, and is cut down; he fleeth also as a shadow, and continueth not.

C., V. C. and *P. C.* All flesh is as grass, and all the glory of man as the flower of the grass. The grass withereth, and the flower thereof falleth away. But the word of the Lord endureth forever.

V. C. We brought nothing into the world, and it is certain we can take nothing out of it.

C., V. C. and *P. C.* The Lord gave, and the Lord hath taken away—blessed be the name of the Lord.

P. C. I know that my Redeemer liveth, and that He shall stand at the latter day upon the earth; and though worms have destroyed this body, yet in my flesh shall I see God, whom I shall see for myself, and mine eyes shall behold and not another.

C., V. C. and *P. C.* God is our God forever; He will be our guide, even unto death.

C. I am the resurrection and the life, saith the Lord; he that believeth in me, though he were dead, yet shall he live, and whosoever liveth and believeth in me shall never die.

[All respond]—O death! where is thy sting?
O grave! where is thy victory?

11th ODE—Air, " King of Peace.'

Clay to clay, and dust to dust,
Let them mingle, for they must ;
Give to earth the earthly clod,
And the spirit unto God.

Never more shall midnight's damp
Darken round this mortal lamp ;
Never more shall noonday light
Glance upon this mortal sight.

Deep the pit and cold the bed
Where the spoils of death are laid ;
Chill the darkness, cold the gloom,
Dwelling in the fearful tomb.

Look aloft, the dust to earth,
Spirit to celestial birth,
Born of God in Heaven above,
Life of light, and joy, and love.

CHAP. Let us pray. Our Father and our God, who art the resurrection and the life; in whom whosoever believeth shall live though he die; and whosoever liveth and believeth in Thee shall not die—hear, we beseech Thee, the voice of Thy creatures here assembled, and turn not away from our supplications.

We humbly beseech Thee so to imbue us with a conviction of our entire helplessness and dependence on Thee, that we may be brought to meditate upon the uncertainty of life, and the certainty of death. In the dispensation of Thy Providence, Thou hast summoned from amongst us our ———, and we, the surviving monuments of Thy mercy, are gathered together to commit ——— remains to the earth. Give, O God, we beseech Thee, Thy Holy Spirit to us, whom Thou hast spared; increase our knowledge, and confirm our faith in Thee forever !

Bless and comfort, we pray Thee, those whom it has pleased Thee to add to the number of the disconsolate. Buoy them up under this heavy stroke; sustain them against despondency. O! wilt Thou be their Father and their God, and pour down from on high Thy blessing upon their heads.

Bless, O Heavenly Father, the brothers and sisters here assembled. Imbue them with the wisdom of Thy laws, and draw
them unto Thee by the cords of Thy irresistible love; impress
them with their duty to each other as brethren and sisters, and
their obligations in the various relations of human life. And
finally, bless our beloved Order throughout the globe. Preserve
its principles and purposes from innovation; sustain it from the
shafts of enmity—protect it from self-innovation, and shield it
from all evil, and unto Thee we shall render all the praise forever—Amen!

2. After the grave is filled, the procession will re-form in the same manner
(except that the sisters may be dismissed to return to their homes in carriages,
or otherwise), and march to the Lodge room, when the Lodge will be closed in
due form, after adopting such resolutions as may be appropriate to the occasion.

INSTITUTING A NEW LODGE.

1. When the Grand Lodge grants a Dispensation or Charter for a new Lodge,
the Grand Chief, Past Grand Chief, Deputy Grand Chief, Chief or Past Chief
to whom the Dispensation or Charter, etc., may be sent, will proceed, with as
little delay as possible, to institute said Lodge. When practicable, the instituting officer should be accompanied by the Grand Marshal or a member of
the Order as D. G. M. At the appointed time, the individuals named in the
Dispensation or Charter, or a sufficient number of them being present, the instituting officer will take the chair, call to order, and say:

G. C. Ladies and Gentlemen (Applicants): I have the
pleasure of announcing that your application to the Grand
Lodge Knights of Jericho of the State of ———, for a Charter
to open a new Lodge, to be hailed as "—— Lodge K. of J.,"
of the State of ———, and located at this place, has been
granted—and I meet you here this ———, for the purpose of or-
ganizing your Lodge, and giving you proper instructions. I
now claim your attention, while I read to you the Dispensation,
which will define your rights and privileges, as well as entitle
you to a Charter soon after your organization. [*Does so.*]

Do you, and each of you, acknowledge the existence of an Almighty God, the Supreme Ruler of the Universe, to whom we are all accountable here and hereafter, and the divinity of the Lord Jesus Christ? [*I do.*]

. In the presence of that great and good Being, are you willing to enter into a solemn covenant with the brothers and sisters of this Order, to abstain from, and discourage the use, as a beverage, of all intoxicating liquors, during your connection with the Order, and so conduct yourself through life as to retain your good name, and not bring the Order into disrepute; and that you will conform to the Constitution, Laws and Regulations of the Order, and do all that within you lies to sustain and carry out the same? [*I am.*]

2. The Grand Chief will cause all who answer in the negative to retire— after which he will obligate and instruct those who answer affirmatively, and then proceed with the organization by requiring the members to elect their officers, afterwhich he will install the same, etc.

G. C. Brothers, you will now please make your nominations, and then proceed to elect the officers of your Lodge. Without any desire to dictate to you in this respect, you will allow me to suggest the great importance of placing none in office, however humble it may be, who cannot, or will not, give a proper degree of attention to its duties.

3. The members of the new Lodge make their nominations, commencing with the Chief. After which, they will proceed to elect them by written ballot. The result of the ballot having been stated by the instituting officer, he will say :

G. C. I now, in the name, and by the authority of the Grand Lodge of ———, declare this Lodge Knights of Jericho legally and constitutionally instituted. The next business in order is the installation of your officers. [Which he proceeds to do, agreeably to the form laid down—omitting the usual ceremony as to entrance of Grand Officers.]

INSTALLATION.

The installation must be performed by the Grand Chief and Grand Marshal or their deputies. When this cannot be done, any Past Chief and Marshal of a Subordinate Lodge may perform the duty. If the installation is to be performed in a church or other public building, the procession must be formed at the Lodge-room and marched to the place where the ceremony is to be performed. On reaching the church, or other place, the procession will be seated by the Grand Marshal, who will conduct the Installing Officer to the chair, and the Junior Past Chief to one on his left. If the installation is held in the Lodge-room, the Grand Officers must be escorted into the Lodge from the ante-room by the Past Chief. On their entrance, the Chief will call up. The Grand Officers will proceed to the altar and salute; the Past Chief will introduce them to the Lodge, while at the altar, when the Lodge will be called down. The Past Chief will then conduct them to seats—the Grand Chief taking the chair of the Chief, and the Grand Marshal that of the Herald. The out-going Chief will occupy a seat at the left of the Grand Chief. On taking the chair, the Grand chief will say:

G. C. Brothers and Sisters: Our business here this——— is to install the officers elect of ——— Lodge Knights of Jericho. [*Turning to the P. C. on his left.*] Have they been constitutionally elected, and all the requisitions complied with?

P. C. They have.

G. C. The Secretary will announce their names.

2. The Secretary will do as directed, and the Grand Marshal will arrange the officers elect in a semi-circle in front of the Installing Officer.

G. C. The officers elect will divest themselves of Regalia, and deliver them, etc., to the Grand Marshal. [*Calls up.*] The brothers and sisters will please sing the 12th Ode.

12th ODE—Air, "Meeting of the Waters."

Now, Brothers and Sisters, thy promise observe;
May faith in each other our union preserve;
Keep each obligation a gem of thy soul—
'Mid every temptation untarnished and whole.

[*After singing, call down.*]

G. M. Sir Knight Grand Chief, the officers elect are now before you, and await your pleasure to be installed.

G. C. Officers elect, will you, in the presence of Almighty God and this assemblage, pledge your word of honor as Knights of Jericho, that you will attend to and strictly perform the duties of the offices into which you are now about to be installed? [Each answers, "I will."]

G. C, Are you ready to be installed? [Each answers, "I am."]

G. C. Sir Knight Grand Marshal, you will make the proclamation.

G. M. Sir Knights and Sisters, you will please take notice that the Grand Chief is now about to install the officers of ———— Lodge Knights of Jericho, of the State of ————. Has any Knight or Lady of Jericho good reason why any one of these officers'elect should not be installed? [*Pauses a moment, and if no objection is urged, he will say:*] Sir Knight Grand Chief, the officers elect of ———— Lodge are now in the position to take the obligation, and they await your pleasure to administer the same. ,

G. C. [*Rises.*] Officers elect of ———— Lodge: You are now about to take upon yourselves a most solemn and binding obligation. You have been elected by your brothers and sisters to fill responsible stations among them. It is of the greatest importance that you should discharge the duties of the same with fidelity. Too often officers become negligent of their duties, and violate a very sacred trust. We cherish the hope that your conduct as officers will be such as will justify the good opinion formed of you, and the more endear you to your worthy brothers and sisters. [*Calls up.*] You will each raise your right hand, so as to form an angle, and repeat after me the obligation, first severally pronouncing your own names.

I, ———, pledge my sacred honor that as an officer of ———
Lodge, I will faithfully and impartially discharge the duties
devolving on me to the best of my ability—that I will support
the Constitution and By-Laws of ——— Lodge, the Constitution and By-Laws of the Grand Lodge of ———, and such
rules and regulations as I shall be made acquainted with from
time to time. I furthermore pledge myself never to expose, or
cause to be exposed, to any person or persons not members of
the Order, any private books or papers entrusted to my care;
that I will not take a copy of the private books or papers, or
any part thereof, nor suffer any person to do so, if in my power
to prevent it, unless specially authorized for the benefit of the
Order; and that I will deliver all and every kind of the private
work and property of the Lodge to my successor in office, or to
the Grand Chief or his deputy whenever demanded. To all the
foregoing I pledge my sacred honor as a Knight of Jericho.

G. C. The brothers and sisters will sing the 13th Ode.

13th ODE—Air, "Hebron"—"Duke Street."

Oh! give us grace, Almighty King!
Unwavering at our post to stand,
Till grateful to Thy shrine we bring
The tribute of a ransomed land;

Which, from the pestilential chain
Of foul Intemperance gladly free,
Shall spread an annal, free from stain,
To all the nations, and to Thee!

[*Calls down, when all will be seated.*]

G. M. Sir Knight Grand Chief, the officers, having been obligated, now await your further pleasure.

G. C. Brothers and Sisters in Office: You have voluntarily
entered into a solemn obligation, faithfully to perform the duties
devolving upon you, in the several offices to which your brothers
and sisters have elected you. The interest of the Order gecer-
ally, and especially your Lodge, demands of you a faithful and
impartial administration of the laws of the Order.

Though office be the just reward of virtue, it is the most severe ordeal to which it can be subjected. Here Honor and probation go together. He who has risen to office has done well, but he who has risen *in* office has done much better.

It will be your duty to see that your brothers and sisters conform themselves strictly to the rules and regulations of the Order. Be kind, courteous and candid in your intercourse with your brothers and sisters, and, by all means, endeavor to promote and preserve harmony in all the transactions of your Lodge—so that, when your several terms of office shall have expired, your brothers and sisters may ever remember with gratitude, and speak commendably of the faithful, just and impartial manner in which you have performed the trust which they have confided to you, and that they may have it in their power to point with confidence to you, and ask your successors to imitate the good example set by you.

You may rest assured, that in entering upon your duties you have my best wishes for your success. The Grand Marshal will invest the officers with their appropriate insignia.

G. M. [*Clothes the officers.*] Sir Knight Grand Chief, your order is executed.

G. C. Sir Knight Grand Marshal, you will please present the Chief.

3. The Grand Marshal will escort the new Chief to the left of the G. C., and say :

G. M. Sir Knight Grand Chief, I have the pleasure of presenting to you brother ———, Chief of ——— Lodge Knights of Jericho.

G. C. [*Takes the C.'s hand.*] It gives me much pleasure to place you at the head of your Lodge. Yours is the most honorable, as it is the most responsible station in the Lodge. I now place in your hands the private work of every kind belonging to your Lodge, and charge you not to forget that you are responsible for their safe keeping. You will please be seated at my left for the present. [*Calls up the officers.*]

4. The G. M. will conduct the several officers around the hall to their respective stations.

G. C. Brethren in office: I need not say to you that the prosperity of your Lodge depends almost entirely upon the faithful discharge of your duties. Your brethren did not elevate you to office to gratify your own ambition, but that the best interests of your Lodge and the Order might be attained. [*Call up the members.*]

Brothers and Sisters: The officers of your choice are now installed, and ready to enter upon the duties of their respective offices. It is your duty, as it should be your pleasure, to give them all the assistance they may require, and that you will never lose sight of the solemn Knightly pledge you have taken to promote the harmony, advance the interests and keep unsullied the reputation of your Lodge and the Order. [*Calls down.*]

5. If the Chief has anything to say, he will now address the audience. The Grand Chief, if disposed, will likewise do so.

G. C. Officers, Brothers and Sisters : The work of installation is complete. We will now take our leave of you, and before we part permit me to tender you my thanks for the polite manner in which you have treated the Grand Officers. May God bless you ! [*Retires.*]

6. If the ceremony has taken place in a public building, the Chief then calls up, and orders the procession to re-form and return to the Lodge-room in the same order in which it came. If the ceremony has taken place in the Lodge-room, they proceed with the regular order of business.

FORM OF RECEIVING OFFICERS.

The officers that are to be received with honors are: The Past and present Grand Chiefs, the Deputy Grand Chiefs, the Past and Present Chiefs.

The officer visiting will give the usual signal at the second gate, and inform the Guard who is in waiting to visit the Lodge, and name his position in the Order. The Guard will announce him to the Chief, who will send out the Past Chief to escort him in. When they enter, the Chief will call up, and the members will sing the following Ode:

14th ODE—Air, "Scotland."

All hail the occasion that bids us rejoice,
Our brothers to welcome, exalt high each voice;
Our work is progressing; this labor of love
Will bring down a blessing from mansions above.

After the usual salutations are given, the Past Chief will introduce the visiting officer to the Chief, and he to the Lodge, as follows: "Officers, Brothers and Sisters, I have the honor to present to you Sir Knight ———" (name the office). On no consideration shall the Chief neglect to receive all the above named officers, unless they decline the honor. The Chief will call down and request the visiting brother to take a seat with him.

.

APPENDIX.

REGALIA.

SEC. 1. The following Regalia shall be common to all members of the Order—male and female: A *Badge*, not exceeding five inches in diameter, outside to outside, to be worn on the left breast—made of material, form and colors as follows: Scarlet material, within a white circle, of width about one-twelfth the diameter of the scarlet center, with an outside border of sky-blue material, not less than three times the width of the white; the same to be plaited or fluted, to resemble a rosette. The scarlet center to contain a five-pointed star of white material or metal, whose extreme points shall be three-fourths the diameter of the scarlet center.

SEC. 2. The male members shall also wear a scarf over the right shoulder, crossing the breast and back to the left hip, not exceeding five inches in width, outside to outside, made of scarlet material, with a white cord or braid one-twelfth the width of the scarlet center, inside a border of sky-blue material three times the width of the white cord or braid.

SEC. 3. In addition to the above, the male members—in Lodge or on parade—shall wear a belt made of red material, (patent or enameled leather preferred), with white metal or embossed star in center of front, provided with small sword and scabbard on left hip.

INSIGNIA.

The Insignias of Grand and Subordinate Officers shall be as follows—those of the Grand Officers to be of yellow, and those of the Subordinate Officers white material or metal:

GRAND OFFICERS.

1. Grand and Past Grand Chief and Deputy Grand Chief (when on duty)—the Sun.
2. Grand Vice Chief—the Crescent.
3. Grand Chaplain—a Sacred Cross, with a five-pointed star to the right, above the Cross.
4. Grand Secretary—Pen and Key, crossed with a five-pointed star above.
5. Grand Marshal—two Straight Swords, crossed with a five-pointed star above.
6. Grand Guard—two Lances, crossed with a five-pointed star above.
7. Elective Members of Grand Lodge—a five-pointed star.

OFFICERS OF SUBORDINATE LODGES.

1. Chief and Past Chief—the Sun.
2. Vice Chief—a Crescent.
3. Preceptress—a scarlet silk Sash, light material, worn as a scarf over the right shoulder, (where it must be secured by a blue and white rosette—center sky-blue) across the front and back to the left hip, the ends ornamented with deep, heavy white fringe, and depending not less than twenty inches below the hip. She may, at her option, wear a wreath representing a crown.
4. Chaplain—a Sacred Cross, with a five-pointed star above.
5. Secretary—two Pens crossed, star above.
6. Treasurer—two Keys crossed, star above.
7. Marshal—two Straight Swords crossed, star above.
8. Herald—a Ram's Horn.
9. Guard—two Lances crossed, star above.
10. Sentinel—two Guns crossed, star above.

All the above described insignia are to be worn on the right breast, attached to the scarf described in Section 3, Regalia, which must be worn by Grand and Subordinate Officers and members of the Grand Lodge; and officers may, at their option, decorate the same by braid and heavy fringe, about three inches deep, and not exceeding five inches long at the shoulder, in imitation of an epaulette—color of fringe white or yellow, to suit Grand or Subordinate Lodge, as the case may be—and, also, at their option, wear a scarlet military sash around the waist, when on duty, or on parade.

The Mourning Badge shall be simply a piece of black crape, formed into a bow or rosette, and worn attached to the badge first described.

On all occasions when members appear in public, in processions, parades or at funerals of members, they are recommended to dress with as much uniformity as convenient or possible; and on such occasions officers may, at their option, wear a cocked hat, with tri-colored feather, in imitation of ostrich feather.

www.ingramcontent.com/pod-product-compliance
Lightning Source LLC
Chambersburg PA
CBHW021601270326

41931CB00009B/1327